The Valley Girls' Guide to Life

Written and Illustrated by *Mimi Pond*

A DELL TRADE PAPERBACK

Lovingly dedicated to my parents,
Janet and Philip Pond

ACKNOWLEDGMENTS

Without the hilarious observations of Leah Pritchard, Kim Hosek, and Melissa Chappell, I could never have begun to write this book. Other such helpful wags include Sande Buhai, Hilary Chester, Susan Fitzpatrick, Emily Hanchett, Margaret Luten, and my brothers, Arthur and Les S. Pond. I am grateful to them all.

A DELL TRADE PAPERBACK
Published by
Dell Publishing Co., Inc.
1 Dag Hammarskjold Plaza
New York, New York 10017

ISBN: 0-440-59334-4

Printed in the United States of America
Fourth printing—January 1983

CONTENTS

LIKE, WHEN YOU GO SHOPPING AND YOUR FRIEND
WHO'S LIKE SUPER-NICE BUT WHO'S GOT THIS
WEIGHT PROBLEM, TRIES ON THIS OUTFIT THAT'S
TOTALLY **GRODY** ON HER AND THE SALESGIRL
TRIES TO CONVINCE HER THAT IT'S BITCHEN.
BARF ME OUT, LIKE I AM SURE.

PRIORITIES: CLOTHES AND DUDES

*S*hopping is the funnest thing to do, 'cause, o.k., clothes? They're important. Like for your image and stuff. I mean you don't want people to think you're some kind of spaz. Like, I'm sure. You have to look good. Everything has to match. Like *everything*. Like your earrings and your shoes and all your accessories and stuff. And you don't want to wear stuff that people don't wear. People'd look at you and just go, "Ew, she's a zod, like get away." And you have to brush your hair a lot in case any guys walk by.

Even if you don't have much billies, you can go hang out with your friends anyway and check out the dudes. Here's something you can buy if you don't have hardly any money: lipgloss, cause you *always* need lipgloss. I mean anyway you have to buy *something* or everyone will think you're wigged out.

You always have to go with at least three other friends, like your best friend and then maybe April and Shawn and Michelle. EVERYONE has to help you decide what to buy. You can't get it unless they say it's super darling on you. 'Cause how would you know by yourself? Like, I'm sure. Sometimes if you don't like one of the girls who's with you, you can get her to buy something totally grody. Then you always look better than she does.

YOU CAN ONLY TRUST YOUR FRIENDS...

All the shops like Judy's and Fashion Conspiracy and Charlotte Russe have real bitchen clothes but the girls who work there are total rags. Real beasties, like not from the Valley or anything. What Yvette and Danielle and me like to do is try on all this stuff we'd *never* buy and make the salesgirl keep bringing us belts and stuff. Then you tell them how ugly everything is and like how come they don't have anything good? Then you ignore them. Another good thing to do is pretend you're from somewhere else like New York or Europe or something and put on a fake accent.

I mean really the only reason we do it is not to be mean or anything, but just to excite our day. Make it fun, you know? Otherwise we might be known as boring people.

The other thing about the mall is all these dudes hang out there too. So you can sit on the planters and stuff and wink at them, or go, real loud, like you're talking to your friend, "GOD, WHAT A CUTE DUDE, HUH?" Or you just laugh real loud. Then sometimes they come over and talk to you, and maybe you exchange phone numbers or something.

If you do that, you always tell the dude opposite names. Like you said you were Heather and she said she was you. That way you call the dude and say it's your friend except it's you. Like you say it's April, 'cause that's really you except he thinks it's your friend. Then you go, "Do you like Heather? 'Cause she thinks you're a vicious babe." That way you find out if they like you. Then later if you go the beach with him or something—it doesn't matter 'cause usually he just thinks he was confused.

Here's another way. Say you're at Chuck E. Cheese and you see a foxy babe. O.K., you get a napkin and write a note on it with lipgloss and take it to him and you say your friend gave it to you to give to him. Then maybe he calls you.

My friend Missy does this. I think it's gross. Ball-watching. That's where you stare at the dude's crotch to freak him out, then you go to your friend, you go, "HOW DOES HE STACK IT?" Real loud, which means do they all hang over to one side or something. *That's* pretty immature though.

CUTE DUDES

O.K., like, first off, if you can't even tell yourself if a dude is cute, you must be a real melvin. I mean everyone knows that Leif Garrett and John Schneider and Andy Gibb and Tom Selleck are maximum brilliant awesome babes.

Well, I don't know about you, but I like would *never* go for a guy that had Sears Toughskin jeans or something. I go more for the guys with Levi's or OPs. Designer jeans, oh, god, they're for goobers. I mean, they're not up to standard.

Okay, if you're going out with a dude and you like decide that he's not as cute as you thought he was, but he's really nice? All you have to do is make all your friends say he's totally cute and then he will be. A dude being cute is way more important than his personality because, god, if he's all bagged out and kind of skanky or something, how's anyone gonna even know that he's super-nice or something? I mean, you know, why you're going with such a dudley-looking guy. They're all gonna just go, "Ew, gross, who's that dude with *her*, man?"

Cute Dudes*

THE CUTEST DUDES HAVE BLOND HAIR, KIND OF LONG, O.K.? IT CAN BE SHORT BUT **ONLY** IF IT'S CUT PUNK, LIKE THE POLICE OR SOMETHING, BUT **NEVER** LONGER THAN SHOULDER-LENGTH. O.K, MAYBE, BUT ONLY IF THE DUDE IS A BIG **VAN HALEN** FAN—AND **THEN** ONLY IF HE'S SUPER-NICE.

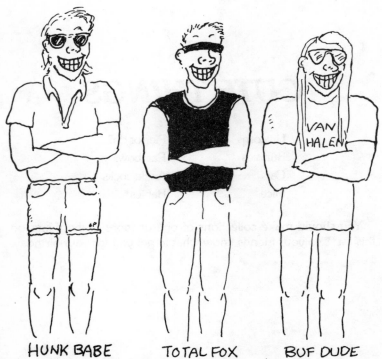

HUNK BABE   TOTAL FOX   BUF DUDE

***DUDES** ARE THE SAME AGES AS VALLEY GIRLS. **GUYS** ARE OLDER THAN DUDES. A VALLEY GIRL MIGHT GO OUT WITH A GUY, BUT SHE WOULD **NEVER** DATE A **MAN.**

VALLEY GIRL STATUS

Health club membership
Atari Home Video Games
Vans Sneakers
A horse
A cool pet like a Shih Tzu

A really bitchen cruisemobile
    like a Vette or a Porsche
Lots of gold jewelry
A monthly clothes allowance
    from your parents

CUTE THINGS

Unicorns
Bunnies
Cats
Mice

Pierrot dolls
Rainbows
Ankle socks
Babies*

   You should make collections of one or more of the things on this list** so your friends know what to get you for your birthday.

*Babies are cute, except when they, like, cry, you know?
**Except for babies.

NECESSITIES

O.K., this is different from status stuff—this is stuff you like *have* to have so nobody thinks you're a zod.

- Curling Iron
- Blowdryer
- Walkman
- Moped
- Your own phone
- Your own stereo
- Personalized license plates
- A double waterbed
- Your own bathroom
- At least ONE gold chain
- A boyfriend (doesn't matter who, just as long as you can say you've got one)
- Knowing one guy who likes you who you'd never go out with

A VALLEY GIRL
BEDROOM

*Y*our bedroom is, like, your own personal space. Kind of your environment, huh? Anyway everything has to be mondo mega cool so you can entertain your friends, 'cause who wants to hang out in the living room, which is where your stupid brother is. Anyway you have private things to discuss, like that totally foxy new babe in your Spanish class, or how come Jeff and Kirstie broke up.

1. Rainbow mobile
2. A totally awesome sound system
3. All your cosmetics out so you can have everything at your fingertips
4. Perfume and lipgloss and nailpolish go in little baskets everywhere
5. Unicorns are totally cool, Stevie Nicks collects them too
6. Windchimes
7. Track lighting is *so* modern
8. Lighted mirror so you can see if you're getting crow's feet
9. Empty Tab cans
10. Pierrot doll
11. Posters of your favorite bands
12. Comforters are in—bedspreads are out
13. If you leave your shoes out, you always know where they are
14. Your own phone is *totally* necessary
15. You *have* to have a waterbed

THE RIGHT CAR

*T*he right car is totally important 'cause it's like an extension of your personality. I mean you can totally tell if someone's a nerd or not by the car they drive. If your parents drive a stupid car, it's almost like death. Just consider yourself lucky if anybody talks to you at all.

Sometimes you can get lucky if your parents get divorced and your dad is going through his second childhood, you know, dating a bunch of babes that're hardly older than you and stuff. 'Cause then he might buy a cool car to impress them, and if you can get him to feel guilty about making you the product of a broken home, he'll let you borrow it. Ten to one it's a Datsun Z car, but sometimes they really get into it and do the full sesh with a Vette or an Alfa or something. *Then* you're cruising.

The only acceptable cars for dudes to drive are Trans Ams, four-wheel drive vehicles, pickups, sports cars, or turbo . . . turbo anything, I think, is cool. Any color but black for guys is too bu-fu.

Girls get to drive cute little foreign cars, like Fiats or Toyotas or Datsuns, but Mercedes and BMWs and Alfas are better. Good girl colors are red, yellow, powder blue, beige, or white. I'm only telling you this stuff for your own good.

Oh, yeah, and obviously, in case you didn't know, your car should be totally equipped with an awesome stereo system. One with lots of dials that looks like it's going to eject your seat and leave oil slicks behind you is the best. And of course you *have* to have personalized plates, like KISME or CATSMEO for girls, and 10 INCH for dudes. Otherwise you're nowhere.

RIGHT CAR

WRONG CAR

SKANKY CARS

*Y*esterday I'm sitting in the living room waiting for Erin and her mom to pick me up to go to Northridge Fashion Mall. So I hear this horn honk and I look out the window and I see this BOAT. I couldn't believe it. Like a STATION WAGON, in *our* driveway, like from 1969 or something. And PINK. Oh, my god. And there's Erin's mom at the wheel. So I go out there and Erin is, like, lying on the floor of the car. Her mom is screaming, "Erin, SIT UP, for god's sake!" Erin is freaking out, going, "No, I'm too EMBAR-RASSED!" I go, "Mrs. Stewart, what happened?" It turned out, O.K., that this was a loaner car while their BMW was in the shop. Then Erin's mom made us actually *sit up* to drive to the mall and I just know all these people saw us. God, where my mom goes to have the car fixed, they at least give you a Fiat. Anyway, *my* mom would've let us stay on the floor.

VALLEY GIRL LIBIDO

*Y*ou know what? Like, O.K., you're supposed to be really into sex and stuff. Like everyone I know totally just talks about it all the time like it's cool to go, "God, I'm *so* horny." But, god, when you really think about it it's just ICKY! I mean, who'd WANT TO? Like everyone talks about how they know, O.K., that, um, Jessica and Garrett are doing it and they almost got caught, but nobody would ever admit to it themselves. That's how you know it's gotta be kinda gross. Except dudes always want to do it. O.K., like I went out with this guy Scott and my best friend (well, she was, but not anymore) Cheryl, and her boyfriend, this dude named Rick, and these guys, god, they wanted to do it in the car. Gross me out! Like, it was a FIAT. I mean, I'M SO SURE. O.K., maybe, in a Trans Am, but only if the dude is a total babe.

At the Beach, Huh...

YOU HAVE TO GO TO THE BEACH WITH **AT LEAST** **TWO** OTHER GIRLFRIENDS...

... THAT WAY IT DOESN'T LOOK SO MUCH LIKE YOU'RE SCAMMING ON THE DUDES.

MAKE SURE YOU FIND TOTALLY VICIOUS BABES TO SIT NEXT TO...

...OTHERWISE SOME MONDO SKANKY MELVIN MIGHT SIT NEXT TO **YOU.**

NEVER GO IN THE WATER — WELL, MAYBE ONCE OR TWICE A YEAR, TO GET A DUDE'S ATTENTION.

IF YOU **DO** GO IN THE WATER, TAKE YOUR BRUSH WITH YOU — USE IT AFTER EVERY WAVE.

–THINGS TO DO AT THE BEACH–

DO YOUR NAILS...

...PUT ON MAKE·UP...

...PUT ON TANNING OIL...

...GO TO THE SNAK WAGON AND MAC·OUT
ON FROOTY PATOOTIES...

...ACT COOL.

BEST-LOVED
VALLEY GIRL NAMES

Heather	Jennifer	Shawn	Christine
Yvette	Barbie	Shaun	Kirs
Elisa	Regan	Shana	Kirsten
Katy	Missy	Melissa	Leanne
April	Danielle	Renee	Cheryl
Megan	Lisa	Rini	Sonya
Kelly	Shannon	Dina	Teri
Cassandra	Sascha	Chrissie	Alexis
Tammy	Shauna	Christie	
Tascha	Sean	Chris	

BEST-LOVED
VALLEY DUDE NAMES

Shane	Ben	Mark	Eric
Shaun	Brandon	Joseph	Chris
Shawn	Jason	Garrett	Scott
Sean	Vance	Clark	Matt
Rick	Lance	Brian	Lief
Darryl	Greg	Brad	Garin

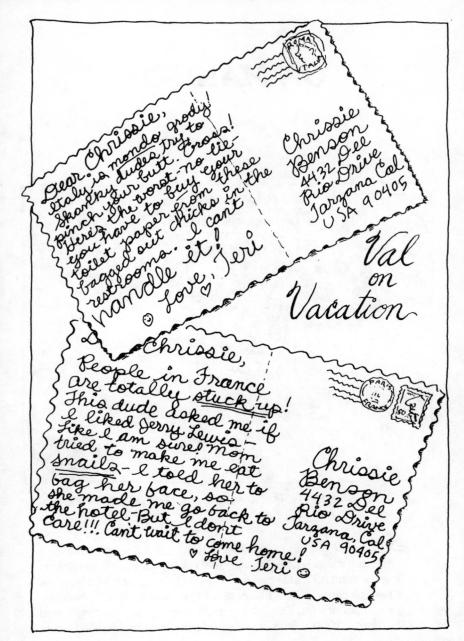

ON MAKE-UP

SHOPPING FOR MAKE-UP IS **TOTALLY FUN**.

So Chrissie got this moisturizer at Robinson's, I forgot what kind it was, but it was real expensive, like, I don't know, like fifty dollars or something for a little tiny jar. She said it cost that much because it had placenta in it. "Placenta," I go, "what's that?" And she goes, "Um, it's . . ." and she gets all embarrassed and stuff, and she goes, "It's this stuff in your body that a baby feeds on when it's in your stomach," and I go "EEWW, GROSS, you're going to put it on your FACE?" And she goes "Well, god, it's got protein, and it's for crow's feet." So I go, "How can you have crow's feet? You're only fifteen." God, she is so dumb. O.K., like, so you don't need moisturizer when you're fifteen. You need toner and foundation and face powder and blusher and shadow and liner and mascara and cleansing cream and stuff like that but no way do you need moisturizer, especially with placenta in it. That is gross. O.K., like Sharma was using this conditioner with that in it, and I told her what it was and, like, she almost barfed.

CONTENTS OF A VALLEY GIRL'S PURSE

*V*alley Girls like really cute, little purses with long skinny straps. If they don't have that kind, they have Velcro clutches that they can get their charge cards out of real fast. You couldn't live without any of this stuff, it's, like, mandatory, O.K.?

1. Flavored lipgloss: At least three—one that's a roll-on, one that's got a wand applicator, and one in a little pot. The wet look is very important
2. One compact with a mirror
3. Two pairs of sunglasses, one sexy with big round rims, and one cool, with mirrored lenses
4. One comb
5. One brush
6. One pair dolphin shorts, 'cause you never know when you'll need them and they fold up real small
7. A lot of barrettes
8. One Rubik's Cube keychain
9. One teeny beach-thong keychain
10. One make-up kit
11. One bottle clear nailpolish for nail emergencies
12. One Velcro wallet with a picture of a sea gull or a sunset on it (Inside the wallet are pictures of all your friends so everyone will know how popular you are. Also, your ID card and maybe your friends' ID's and definitely your boyfriend's.)
13. One purse-size perfume—White Shoulders or Love's Baby Soft or Chantilly or Babe
14. A bunch of rubber bands
15. One pack Bubblicious or Carefree sugarless (strawberry flavor)

PLAYING HARD-TO-GET

VALLEY GIRL Q AND A

Q. *If you could buy only one thing in a day of shopping, what would it be?*

A. One thing? Are you an airhead or something? That's what credit cards are for.

Q. *Which school is better, University of California at Santa Barbara or Harvard?*

A. What, are you a zod? UCSB has the beach right there and way more parties. Isn't Harvard in Philadelphia or something? Someplace where it's cold, anyway.

Q. *Which beach is better, Venice or Zuma?*

A. Are you totally kidding? Like did you have too many Heinies before lunch or something? I mean are you a geek? Anybody knows that a Val would get her butt kicked by the surfers and the stoners at Venice, where everything is totally skanky. Anyway, Malibu is way cooler.

Q. *What's more fun—going to Europe or going to the Galleria?*

A. Are you nuts? They don't even speak English in Europe. How could you buy anything?

Q. *What does a Valley girl think about during the Act of Love?*

A. Huh?

Q. *Why is a tan important to a Val?*

A. I'm sorry, but if you wear white without a tan, you just look terminal, that's all. God, you ask stupid questions.

Q. *What is the Number One problem of Valley girls?*

A. O.K., like, you may not believe this 'cause we have this reputation for being total babes, but I'll tell you: cellulite. *Everyone's* really worried about it. I mean you could be totally skinny and it's *still there.* Like this gross cottage cheese stuff on your legs. It's getting serious, man. I think maybe pollution causes it. It makes dudes hate you, too.

A GNARLY SITUATION: YOU'RE AT A
FOREIGNER CONCERT. YOUR BEST FRIEND
BORROWS YOUR LIPGLOSS AND DROPS IT IN THE
TOILET BY ACCIDENT, LIKE BEFORE YOU GOT A
CHANCE TO USE IT. GROSS, **TOTALLY**.

VALLEY GIRL DIPLOMACY: YOU'RE AT A FOREIGNER CONCERT. YOUR BEST FRIEND BORROWS YOUR LIPGLOSS AND DROPS IT IN THE TOILET BY ACCIDENT, LIKE BEFORE YOU GOT A CHANCE TO USE IT—BUT HER BROTHER IS A TOTALLY AWESOME BABE.

Q. *What is the Number One quality a Val looks for in a dude?*

A. Well, dudes have *got* to be totally buf, first off, before you even talk to them. O.K., like, you wouldn't just buy an outfit 'cause it's warm, right? You'd want it to be in fashion and stuff. And it has to fit, right? It's the same with dudes. I mean there's plenty of nice *ugly* guys around but how many nice hunks are there? Let's face it, all a dude is interested in is the bod, like they don't even care if *you're* nice. Who are you asking all these questions for, anyway, Spaz Digest or something?

Q. *Aren't leg warmers too warm to wear in the San Fernando Valley, where temperatures rarely drop below fifty degrees?*

A. Comfort has totally nothing to do with fashion, or haven't you noticed, you honker.

Q. *What is the biggest status symbol among your peer group?*

A. Status symbol? Um, let's see, last year it was mink jackets, but those are totally joanie now. The coolest thing to have is a diamond ring. Anything below a half carat is unacceptable, totally. Meagan at school has a carat and a half, but that's 'cause her dad's on a guilt trip. I think they're a way better investment than mink jackets, anyway. God, like I tried to sell mine at our garage sale, and nobody wanted to pay more than $75 for it, and like it cost $350. What, are you from the welfare department or something? Look, my mom and dad are divorced, but he sends the check every month and I see him on weekends. I don't know what that space-cadet shrink at school told you, but . . . What's a peer group, anyway? They already told me those tests didn't really mean anything, like IQ doesn't even count.

Q. *Do a Val and her mom get along better than other teen-agers and their mothers?*

A. Did you like have a little Bud sesh before you got here? I mean, you have *got* to be kidding. Like my mom, she thinks she's so cool just 'cause she wears designer jeans and borrows my tops, but she still makes me do this gross stuff that I personally would not even make our dog do. Like, I told her I wasn't into housework, and she said she didn't want to deprive me of the joy of sharing the experience with her. Ever since she took est she's been a pain in the butt.

Q. *What do you want to be when you grow up?*

A. GROW UP? I am grown up, you melvin. I already wear a size and a half bigger shoe than my mom. How am I supposed to know what I want to be? I mean, I don't even plan my outfits more than a day in advance—except I always know what I'm going to wear on the last day of school. Every year I start planning it around Christmas time. I've been doing that since, like, fifth grade. See, that way, you leave this impression on people. Like they remember you looked good. But I don't know what I want to *be*. Dina says she's going to be a model, like she went to modeling school—but now all she does is practice walking funny. Like I'm SURE.

Q. *Why do you wear a headband?*

A. Like for the opposite reason you wear that skanky shirt, you nerd. So I'll look good. Are you almost done with these questions?

Q. *Do you think your reputation really counts?*

A. Are you zee'd out? Anybody knows that dudes are totally unpredictable. I mean you never know what they're going to do from one minute to the next. I mean they talk. So you have to be careful. Like don't you worry about your rep? I mean, you should hear what we say about dudes.

Q. *Do you have any advice for teen-agers?*

A. Yeah, like it's important to be practical. Like getting your hair done so that you can wear it more than one way. Otherwise it gets boring and you have to wait for it to grow out. And it's worth paying more for a good cut, 'cause if you get a bad one, it's mondo depressing. Like my friend Jessica, she wouldn't come out of her room for a week 'cause she was so bummed out. I mean, it really *did* look spazzy, but we told her it looked O.K.—uh-oh, is this going to be on the tape? If she hears I said that, she'll kill me. Is this the end? O.K., so you'll cut that part out? O.K.

Valley Girl Philosophy

IF YOU'RE SERIOUS, YOU CAN'T HAVE FUN!

PEOPLE SAY WE'RE IMMATURE, BUT WE DON'T CARE!

DO I LOOK OKAY?

Valley Girl Gestures

O.K. SO YOU'RE JUST KIND OF STANDING THERE, RIGHT?

GOD, TUBULAR!

O.K., SO YOU FIND OUT YOU WON TICKETS TO SEE JOURNEY.

GOD, I KNOW, HUH.

YOU CAN DO THIS FOR ALMOST ANY OCCASION.

NO, DUH.

SOME AIRHEAD SAYS SOMETHING LIKE REALLY, TOTALLY STUPID.

SOMEONE, LIKE
PROBABLY A DUDE,
SAYS SOMETHING
TOTALLY GROSS,
AND YOU HAVE TO
GO LIKE YOU'RE
REALLY, MAXIMUM
DISGUSTED THEY
COULD BE SO·O·OO
IMMATURE. BUT,
LIKE, NOT REALLY.

THAT IS **SO ILL.**

THIS IS GOOD FOR THE
TIMES LIKE, OK, YOUR
MOM TELLS YOU YOUR
GOOBER COUSIN NEEDS
A DATE FOR SOME DUMB
DISCO DANCE AT HIS
SCHOOL. BARF ME OUT,
LIKE **NO WAY.**

VALLEY GIRL LIST OF FAVORITES

FAVORITE DIET EXPRESSIONS

Favorite Gross-outs
Belching and burping and farting, which provides comic relief when things get dull—everyone gets to talk about how totally gross it is.

Favorite Soft Drink
Tab, Pepsi Light, Coke, and Mountain Dew.

Favorite Beer
Heineken (Heinies) and Löwenbräu (Lowies).

Favorite Gum Brand
Bubblicious or Carefree sugarless, (strawberry flavor).

Favorite Cosmetics
Alexandra De Markoff.

Favorite Tanning Oil
Hang Ten or Tropical Blend.

Favorite Junk Food
Doritos.

Favorite Fast Food
Anything Mexican, especially burritos.

HERE'S A WAY TO HAVE FUN WHEN THINGS GET DULL: **BELCH.**

Favorite Video Games
Pac-Man and Xaxxon.

Favorite Magazines
People, Creem, Teen, Seventeen, High Times, National Enquirer.

Favorite College Majors
Nutrition and Animal Health Technology.

Favorite Ambitions
Modeling, Fashion Design, Stewardess, *Solid Gold* Dancer.

Favorite Diets
Valley Girls always talk about going on diets, but they never do, really. Their favorite one is where you just eat a million little strawberries or cantaloupe and Tab.

Favorite Beaches
Malibu and Zuma

Fave Hang-outs
The beach, the mall, Malibu Grand Prix, and the 7-Eleven.

Favorite Bumperstickers
I Brake for Unicorns
I ♡ Encino
Too Hip

Fave Bands
Journey, Rush, Van Halen, AC/DC, Foreigner, The Police, The Go-Go's, Rick Springfield, Pat Benatar, Blondie.

Favorite Movie of All Time
Mommie Dearest, 'cause it was kind of sad.

ON DAYS WHEN YOU CAN'T GET TO THE MALL OR THE BEACH: PIGGING OUT ON DORITOS IN FRONT OF THE 7-11 IS ALWAYS FUN.

SLEEP-OVERS

*S*leep-Overs used to be called slumber parties, which is totally stupid. I mean, what's a slumber, anyway. Dumb word, huh? So you get like four friends (if you invite any more than that there's no one left to talk about) to spend the night at your house. Good things to do at your sleep-over:

—Pig out on Doritos and Tab and ice cream
—Make each other up totally punker
—Play Atari and watch HBO or videodiscs of your favorite groups
    What you really *have* to do is talk about everyone you didn't invite, like what ugly clothes they have and stuff. Then everyone says who they love the most, like John Schneider or Matt Dillon or Steve Perry (like I swear he looked *right at me* at the last Journey concert, no, REALLY) and nobody can have dibs on the same guy. Then maybe you talk about whether AC/DC really *does* stand for "Against Christ Devil's Children" or not, and should you still like them anyway?
    O.K., here's the funnest part: You call up some guy like maybe either the cutest or the grisliest dude in the whole school or something and tell him it's some girl who's not at the party, like one you totally can't stand. Then you tell the guy that she's madly in love with him and she's been dreaming of him for months and months and she wants to marry him or something. You go on like that as long as you can without cracking up. If the dude is a complete airhead, sometimes he even believes it. This is good for at least an hour's worth of fun, sometimes even longer if you dare each other who's going to do it.
    Eventually everyone gets in a worse and worse mood 'cause nobody's really used to staying up that late even if they *say* they do it all the time and finally somebody ends up rolfing on too many Doritos or something. Then everyone passes out. In the morning you make your mom get up and make pancakes out of chocolate cake mix and have it with strawberry ice cream. Then everyone goes home feeling yucky. But it's fun.

HIGH SCHOOL

*H*igh school is—like you know how you only get out of it what you put into it? It's like that, kind of. 'Cause your image is totally everything. You have to be into the full buff or people are going to go, "Ew, get away." I mean, noboby *cares* if you make bad grades, but if you come to school all bagged out you might as well forget it. NO WAY are you going to get invited to parties. Being popular is important. Otherwise people might not like you.

Having a boyfriend is MONDO important. When you get a new one, you have to tell everyone like how you're in love and stuff, but then you break up with him after about a week. After that you have to hide when you see him coming in the hall and stuff. If you still have a class with him, it can be really gnarly, like, him or you should just drop out of school completely.

CONVERSATIONS IN VAL-SPEAK

O.K. like if someone's your friend, they're going to know what you're talking about anyway, right? So if you go, "Cruisemobile, wow," like that's enough 'cause they just KNOW you like their car. Or if you go, "Cruised down to the lake," everyone goes, "Wow, you went to the lake, huh," 'cause they like know it's a bitchen place to go. Unless you mean someone else went to the lake. Or that you wanted to go to the lake, but you didn't. Or you're going to go to the lake. Or maybe you went last year or something. It doesn't matter anyway because going to the lake is just a cool thing.

FUN WITH HEADBANDS

HEADBANDS ARE TOTALLY BITCHEN! OLIVIA
NEWTON-JOHN WEARS ONE ALL THE TIME.
I HAVE LIKE ABOUT A **HUNDRED** OF THEM.

O.K. NORMAL,
SEE?

BUT YOU CAN PRETEND
YOU'RE A GOOBER...

OR YOU COULD WEAR
IT UNDER YOUR CHIN
AND PRETEND TO
TALK WITH A FOREIGN
ACCENT AND FREAK
PEOPLE OUT...

OR YOU COULD WEAR IT
DOWN ALMOST IN YOUR
EYES SO PEOPLE THINK
YOU'RE ZEEKED OUT,
WHICH YOU'RE NOT.
FUN, HUH?

BREAKING UP WITH A DUDE: VALLEY STYLE

O.K., this is important 'cause if you don't know how to break up with a dude, you could end up, like, married to him or something. Or the dude you really like instead could end up going with some chick you hate. Which would be totally gnarly, really. But here's some excuses that really work. Tell Him:

1. He's too good for you. This is old but he's not and maybe he hasn't heard it before.
2. You've decided to become a nun. If he asks you why, tell him it's 'cause you look so good in black. Anyway nuns don't have boyfriends.
3. You have to wash your hair.

They say honesty is the best policy, but you don't want to hurt a dude's feelings, right? You can also tell him you want to still be friends but anyone who's not a total airhead *knows* that's mega-bogus. When you break up with a dude, you usually never even talk to them again. It's kind of like they died or something.

COED WEEKEND

*M*y sister Shannon, she's eighteen and she goes to San Diego State. State's a really good school 'cause it's got this total party reputation and it's pretty close to the beach and stuff. I'm going to go there too unless I became a *Solid Gold* dancer or go to stewardess school instead. Shannon is totally bitchen. I mean, I like her a lot more now that she moved away from home. We don't fight as much that way. Like the time I dropped her blowdryer in the pool. Well, god, it WAS an accident. Anyway, Shannon still likes to have fun and freak people out and stuff. Her major is undeclared 'cause she says you can take all these classes like ceramics, and logic, and Dental Health I and meet more dudes that way.

Last weekend Mom let me go visit her and stay in the dorm and everything. It was MONDO party time. The best thing about State is that it is major-babe city. All these foxy dudes, real buf, I mean totally mature, not like the guys at the mall or anything, but with mustaches, O.K.?

God, first it was luau night at this frat that is like the coolest frat at State. I mean they only let the best chicks come to their parties, and Shannon's sorority got invited. They had like ten kegs and plastic leis. Here's what they did when we came in. They put the lei around your neck and they go, "Aloha, Wanna Lei?" I got SO embarrassed, god. The best part was when they threw us in the pool. Then I got tweeked and I rolfed in the bushes, but it was O.K., 'cause everyone was doing it, even the totally foxy dudes.

The next night was designer jean night, O.K., all the chicks have to wear designer jeans and they give a prize to the one with the cutest butt. Except not the dudes, 'cause let's face it, any dude who'd wear designer jeans *must* be bu-fu, right? Then guess what: I won. But they found out how old I was, fourteen, and they got all like, "Ooh, jail bait, man." So they gave the prize to this stuck-up chick named Monique. The prize was black bikini panties. They thought it was totally funny, but *I* got embarrassed. I mean, you HAD to laugh or they'd think you were some kind of zod. I was glad it wasn't me even if I *did* have a cuter butt. Anyway they weren't my size.

Sunday in Shannon's dorm there was a food fight in the cafeteria but everyone got in trouble. Anyway it was all totally more fun than you could have with the usual *children* I hang out with. I used to wonder, but now I KNOW I'm more sophisticated than they are. I can hardly wait till I'm eighteen.

WHEN YOU **REALLY** MEAN IT

THE VALLEY GIRL DICTIONARY

Airhead—Someone totally dumb.

Awesome—Nice, you know, like really totally nice.

Bagged-out—Someone whose clothes are old and not in style or anything and they don't match, which is totally untogether.

Bagpipe It—Forget it.

Bag Your Face—A real put-down, 'cause like bagging something is throwing it away, see.

Bag Z's—Like, sleeping, you know?

Bail—When you skip school and your friends ask you where you were, it's cool to go, "like, I bailed, man." Or when you leave a party you go, "Let's bail."

Barf City—Come on, you know, like, yuck.

Barf Me Out—Like, make me puke, the worst.

Beastie—Someone from somewhere else who doesn't even know what OPs are and is a total jel or something.

A "BEASTIE"
(PROBABLY, HUH)

A "BEIGE" DUDE

Beige—For sure boring.

Billies—Like money.

Bitchen—Totally the best.

Bitchen Twitchen—*More* than bitchen. Mondo bitchen.

Bite the Ice—Like, take a hike.

Blitz—What happens when you party and drink mondo martinis, you get blitzed.

Blow Me Away—Freaking out, except more like, O.K., like a dude who's a mega babe asks you if you want to meet him at the beach tomorrow and you are like blown away 'cause you thought he'd already have a girlfriend, like, wo.

Blow-off—Study hall is a blow-off, real easy.

Bogus—Someone or something that's mega-phony, like this girl I know who thinks she's practically Joan Jett or something.

A TOTALLY BOGUS CHICK, HUH.

Book It—O.K., if you're in a hurry, you go "Wo, like I gotta book it."

Book the Joint—Check it out.

Break-in—O.K., this is kind of hard, you go, "She's a break-in," that means she's leaving.

Bud Sesh—Smoking pot, I mean, if you don't know what that is, you *must* be a geek.

Buf—A strong dude, usually a total fox.

Bummer—Like, a total drag, you know?

Burn—Like, I burned this chick, I go, "Whereja get those jeans, like SEARS or something?"

Buzz—Cruise around in your car.

Buzz the Nab—Like, leave, get away.

A GOOD PUT-DOWN

Cas—Short for casual, but what you say about clothes that are totally cool.

Case It Around—Like, check it out, or do something else or something.

Catch Some Rays—A cooler thing to say than good-bye.

Chill Out—Calm down.

Choice—A choice babe is like Tom Selleck or Rick Springfield, like that.

Clearly—Totally or maximum, or like really.

Completely—Like clearly.

Cool—Like hot.

Cool Out—We told him to cool out in front of my mother and not act so gross.

Cool the Rock—If someone's getting too hyper, you go, "Wo, cool the rock, man."

Cop the Tube—O.K., when you go surfing and catch a totally tubular wave.

Crank—You can use this word for almost anything, like you crank yourself together or you crank to school, or you crank up the radio, kind of an all-purpose word, you know?

Crispy—A burn-out, like someone who does too many 'Ludes or something.

Cruise—O.K., a class in music appreciation is a cruise job, or finding the right belt for a white dress is really cruise, 'cause any color goes with white, or you can just cruise to the beach, or anywhere, you know?

Cruisemobile—A totally cool car, like a 'Vette.

Dick—A grody guy to the max, who thinks he's Mr. Awesome.

Double-Bagger—Someone who looks skanky or grody—like they're so ugly you need *two* bags, one for them and one for you.

Dud—What a dud, you know, like a bummer only more boring.

Dude—Someone who's not a chick, like a guy, you know?

Dudley—A guy who's a dud.

Excellent—What dudes say instead of mega major maximum brilliant, they just go, "Excellent, man."

Fag Your face—Another good put-down, it means like fuck you, man.

Fancy—Really, really good, extra better, kinda.

Forget You—Like, no way!

For Sure—Um, what's the other word for that? Definitely, or sometimes just yes.

Fox—A dude or chick who's a super mondo cool maximum babe and a half.

Freaking Me Out—Sort of like when something weird happens and you don't know how to act, it freaks you out.

Fruit—Someone really stupid.

Full Buf—When you look totally hot with real cas clothes your friends go, "Wo, the full buf, huh."

Full Sesh—When you do the full sesh, you do the whole thing.

Fully—Same as totally.

Gee—Short for gross.

"DICK"   "MEGA·DICK"

MORAL CONFLICT: MEGA·DICK WITH AN AWESOME CRUISEMOBILE

Geek—Someone who is so totally skanky and such a dud that you can't even believe it.

Giving Cone—Like, one of the grossest things you could ever do, it's like barfy just to even *think* about it, O.K., like ORAL SEX, O.K.? Like it grosses me out to even say it.

Go—You know, I go to her, "O.K., if you're so smart, how come you don't even know who Norma Kamali is?" and she goes, "Oh, huh."

Go for it—It's like, um, do something.

Goober—A really dumb guy.

Gotta Blow—Gotta bail, or book it, you know.

Go with the Dirt—Get lost, beat it.

Gnarly—O.K., if you wanted to go to a totally hot concert with a super babe and your mom said you had to stay home and wait for the guy to come fix the hot tub 'cause she had an acupuncture appointment—that would be, like, gnarly.

Grisly—Some dude with zits or someone fat who likes you.

"GRISLY"

Grody—Gross, the worst, but sometimes so gross it's way bitchen, like a horror movie is super grody.

Groovy—Something totally out of date like a peace symbol necklace, you know?

Gross—Grisly or grody, something totally icky.

Gross Me Out—Like being freaked out only more like barf city.

Honker—Someone weird.

Hot—Like cool.

Huh—Sort of agreeing with someone, or just what you say when you're trying to think of what else to say, you go like, "Oh, huh, I'm sure."

Hunk of Beefcake—A dude who's a real buf babe, O.K., like at University Town Centre Mall, my friend Kelly goes, she goes, real loud so the dude can hear her, "I want a piece of that beefcake!"

Hyper—How you get around a dude who's a total babe and you would like freak out if he asked you to go anywhere,

ACTING "HYPER"

especially if he's got an awesome car, like a 'Vette, I mean, you get too, like you talk too much and giggle and stuff and he probably thinks you're a double-bagger anyway. Then you're hyper.

I Am Sure—Like you don't believe it, like do you look stupid or something?

I Am So Sure—Like NO WAY, do they expect you to swallow THAT?

I Can't Handle It—When something is too gross or awesome like maybe a total fox asks you do you want to go to this party, it's like too much, you know?

I Don't Know—Like, I don't know, you know?

I Know—What you say when your girlfriend is telling you something, you go "God, I know, huh."

I'm Stoked—Being totally into something, almost like you can't handle it, because it's sooooo tubular, like when a mega-cute dude asks you to go see Ozzie Ozbourne, you get totally stoked to the max.

Jam—Booking it, when you jam your class you've got to leave fast.

Jel—O.K., like a Jello-brain, someone who's a total geek.

Joanie—Old and stupid and out of date.

Killer—O.K., mostly dudes say this, so it's like excellent.

Kiss My Tuna—EEw, this is totally gross 'cause like who'd want to do oral sex anyway so it's a real good put-down, like ick.

Later—Instead of good-bye, you go, "Later," cool, huh?

Let's Boogie—Like, let's blow.

Let's Get Juiced—Let's get wasted.

Let's Get Wasted—Let's get juiced—O.K., like blitzed, you know, so that at the end you puke your guts out? Like it's fun till that happened.

Lick My Froth—O.K., like kiss my tuna.

Like—What you say when you're like, um, attaching one word to another, in a, like, sentence.

Live—O.K., you go, "She's live," that means she's great.

Mac-out—Pig-out, you know, on pizza or something.

Major—Major cool is clearly the best.

Marv—The opposite of an airhead, someone who you copy off their tests.

Maximum Brilliant—Totally or like really bitchen.

Mega—Totally only even more total than totally—like mega-gross.

Melvin—Creepy, like out in space, like a weird person.

Mondo—Mondo cool max—O.K., a new dress from Fashion Conspiracy is mondo cool max, or like totally, like we did a mondo mac-out.

Mr. Bu-Fu—A gay guy who's real swishy, you know? Like the guy who puts blond highlights in your hair.

No Biggie—Like, don't worry about it.

No, Duh—I'm sure. Like do you think I'm a nerd? Obvious, you know?

No Way—Like forget you.

Oh—A word you use with like.

Oh My God—Just something to say when stuff is weird or you're freaked out, or blown away, you just go, "Oh my god."

Ooh, Base—What you say when someone totally puts down someone else real good, you go, "OOOOh, BASE!"

Ooh, Gross—If you saw someone wearing, like, platform shoes or something like that you'd go, "Ooh, gross." Or if your cat barfed or something.

Outrageous—Like mondo bitchen.

Party—You can go to one or you can just party all by yourself or with your friends, like have a good time.

Pig-out—You know, like mac-out.

PO'ed—When Yvette spilled her tostada all over my white mini, I was totally P.O.'ed 'cause I knew she did it 'cause she was jealous.

Poindexter—Like a marv, someone who reads a lot of books and stuff.

Rad—. . . Where does that word come from? Let's see—oh, yeah, like short for radical, like awesome, or sometimes just anything fun.

Rag—Like, Don't be rag, like stop being a bitch or something.

Ragged Out—Someone who's totally ragged out is totally a rag.

60

Raspy—Like bitchen.

A Real Babe—A Totally cute dude. Or a super cute chick, if you're a dude.

Really—For sure, or maybe totally.

Really Fine—Like the opposite of totally nauseating.

Really Sad—More like an expression that some super-phony girls use when they're trying to pretend they're all nice—like if you said your dog died and they'd go in little teeny voices, "God, that's really sad," and then you go, "Well, my dog died FIVE YEARS AGO," that makes them look dumb.

Really Sweet—What totally bogus chicks say when they're trying to get you to believe that they like someone, they go, "God, she's really sweet."

Real Smart—Real dumb.

THE KIND OF GIRL WHO'D
SAY "REALLY SAD"

Rolf—What always happens to me when I get blitzed, I always rolf in the bushes or someplace really dumb like Monique's mom's carpet, which is totally uncool.

Sap—Someone strange.

Scarf-out—Like pigging-out, the same.

Scruff—My room's always totally scruff, like messed up.

Seeyabye—When you bail, you go, "O.K., seeyabye."

Shred the Tube—A totally cool way to say you're going surfing.

Skanky—A chick or a dude who's a double-bagger.

Slightly Obvious—Like TOTALLY obvious, like even Stevie Wonder could see it.

Space Cadet—Someone who acts like they're on another planet or something.

Spacing—Like you're supposed to be listening to your teacher but instead you're thinking of some total major babe and a half, then you're spacing, see?

Spazzy—You know, someone who's acting like a total spaz, like a zod or a geek.

Super—Kind of like totally, or really, you know, when you really mean it.

Surfed-out—Someone who has like a mega tan and a Town and Country board and is totally into going in the water instead of just catching UVs.

Take It Easy—Like, catch some rays.

Tell Me About It—It's like you already know, like no, duh.

That Is So Ill—Super gross, like when you go see *Humongous,* 'cause you think some foxy dudes will be there that you might meet and stuff, but the movie is so gross like only a dude would like it and you go, "God, that is SO ILL," and the dude thinks it's so fun that you're ready to barf.

Total Blowchoice—Well, kind cool, but really, who cares?

Totally—To the max.

Totally Nauseating—The opposite of really fine.

To the Max—Totally.

Trippy—Like outrageous.

Tubular—If you were a hippie or something, you'd say it was cosmic except nobody says that anymore and tubular sounds more cool, like awesome.

Tweeked—When you get wasted, you're tweeked.

UVs—O.K., that stands for ultra-violet rays, like when you're soaking up the UV's you're getting a tan. Tans are totally important.

Vicious—A totally foxy dude is vicious.

A "VICIOUS" DUDE

A "WARM" BABE

Warm—O.K., a mondo outrageous girl? Dudes call her warm.

Way—A way foxy dude is a total babe. Or a way cute outfit is like totally cute.

Wicked—Real good.

Wigged-Out—Being flipped out or z'ed out, acting totally untogether.

Wo—Like if you're impressed, you go, "Wo, man, like cruisemobile, huh," or something.

Wonelly—Kind of almost tubular, like *Halloween* was a wonelly movie.

Z—Sleep, like, "Gotta Z, man."

Z'd out—When you can't wake up 'cause you slept too much, you're z'd out.

Zeeked Out—Like, acting like a goon, or crazy or something, O.K., like this guy Darryl, he totally zeeked out in front of my mother, and I go, "God, Darryl, what are you, a space-cadet?"

Zod—Someone weird.

Zooned Out—Zeeked out only even worse.